Brecker Bunny Learns to Be Careful!

A Lesson in Fire and Burn Safety

By Hilary D.R. Bilbrey
Illustrated by Michael Rose

Inspired by Family

Brecker Bunny Learns to Be Careful!
Copyright © 2007 by Inspired by Family
Printed in the United States of America. All Rights reserved.
ISBN13: 978-0-9787074-1-5
ISBN: 0-9787074-1-9

Library of Congress Control Number: 2006939899

Graphic Design by Laura Keene - *Keene Insights*.
www.keeneinsights.com

HM Graphics, Inc Milwaukee, WI is proud to be associated with
WAFS and Inspired by Family in the printing of Brecker Bunny Learns To Be Careful.

Published by *Inspired by Family*
To order books or for more information contact
www.InspiredByFamily.com and **www.WAFS.org**

Copyright © 2007 Brecker Bunny's Fire Safety Checklist by Wisconsin Alliance for Fire Safety

Copyright © 2007 Brecker Bunny's Family Calendar Wisconsin Alliance for Fire Safety with Underwriters Laboratories

Copyright © 2007 Brecker Bunny Illustrations Michael Rose

BRECKER BUNNY'S GUIDE

Brecker Bunny Learns to Be Careful is first and foremost a children's book. We hope you cuddle with your child while reading and discuss whatever questions might come up.

For teachers and parents, however, we have included some activities for after you read.

• Notice the *Safety Smart!* in the bottom corner of some of the pages. This corresponds with Brecker Bunny's Safety Tips (provided by UL) immediately following the story. Use these to start discussions after or while you read. Practice the tips together.
Don't use all the tips at once, but cover a few each time you read the story.
• After the tips, you will find a wonderful calendar provided by UL. This calendar will help you remember when to check the different safety devices in your home.
• WAFS has provided an excellent four-page safety checklist for your home at the end of the book. For more tips and extra copies of the checklist, see **www.wafs.org**.
• For more ideas, exercises, tips and activities, see www.inspiredbyfamily.com.

We hope you will find **Brecker Bunny Learns to Be Careful** useful. We are all responsible for helping children make the right choices regarding safety. Our goal is to help prevent fires and burns before they happen. Hopefully our lessons will make that a little easier. Stay safe.

"Please note that the safety tips in back are one page off the actual book page numbers in first editions only."

BRECKER BUNNY'S PARTNERS

Wisconsin Alliance for Fire Safety (WAFS) - www.wafs.org

In a span of fifteen days, three City of Milwaukee fires took the lives of seventeen children and three adults. One fire resulted in the deaths of 12 people. The impetus for the Wisconsin Alliance for Fire Safety began during that fifteen day period in 1987.

Representatives from many organizations met to attempt to find a solution. Simply, the task force analyzed that fire safety education, especially with the youth of the city, would be the key element to reduce tragic fires. As a state, as a city, and as an organization, the lesson learned was that we needed to educate the members of our community from an early age on, in order to prevent a repeat of that tragedy. The Alliance is dedicated to being a fire safety and prevention resource for the State of Wisconsin.

Underwriters Laboratories Inc. (UL) - www.ul.com

Underwriters Laboratories Inc. (UL) is an independent, not-for-profit product safety testing and certification organization. Founded in 1894, as the world's leading product safety testing and certification organization, UL is synonymous with safety. Its UL Mark is the most recognized and trusted symbol of safety in the world. UL tests more than 19,000 types of products, and 20 billion UL Marks appear on products each year.

Consumers and regulatory authorities value UL as a leader on safety issues. With public safety at the heart of UL's mission, UL acts as a safety resource and advocate. UL works closely with customers, regulators, insurers, retailers and consumers on research, technology and safety initiatives. UL also promotes public safety through education and outreach.

UL is dedicated to public safety and committed to working for a safer world.

BRECKER BUNNY SAYS THANK YOU

I would first like to acknowledge my son, Breck. I did not know who I was meant to be until I became his mommy. Watching him make his way in this world fills me with awe and inspires me to strive to become a better person. If I succeed in this life, it will be because my children, Breck, Jake and Faith continually give me the courage to "be the change". To my husband, Jeff, thank you for your unwavering belief. Thank you to my mom for pushing me to write this from a child's perspective. To the rest of my family, I so appreciate your endless hours of encouragement, revision and promotion!

Brecker Bunny may not have come to be without the enthusiasm, dedication and service of Wisconsin Alliance for Fire Safety, specifically Dan and Mary Gengler. Their involvement is not about self promotion, it is about saving one child and every child from having to go through painful burn injuries. In everything that Dan does, he speaks for the voice of every frightened child he ever carried out of a burning building and honors the spirit of every little voice that was forever silenced in the ashes.

Michael Rose, the illustrator, you have only begun to explore your amazing talent! To Laura Keene, the graphic designer, you are, as always, the goddess of efficiency and sanity! You are a superb graphic designer, but an even better mom to Max and Connor! To everyone at UL, especially Ginger Sommer, thank you for caring about our kids and making their safety your mission!

We would be pleased to add your company logo to this space if you would like to donate to our mission. Our goal is to make sure every family with a preschooler in Wisconsin, and eventually the country, will have one of these books. Join us in our mission to make our kids safer. No Child should have to suffer a burn injury. Please contact Wisconsin Alliance for Fire Safety at 1-800-315-0911 or visit www.WAFS.org.

Brecker Bunny likes to dance and sing.
In fact, he likes most anything.

He likes to jump and play and hop.
He likes to twist and turn and bop.

He likes to have adventures in a small tree,
While Little Brother yells, "Wait for me!"

But some adventures are left undone,
Mommy and Daddy tell their little son.

Safety Smar

When things are very hot you should stay away,
Or your paws and whiskers might not be okay.

Be careful of boiling water on the stove,
Or when Farmer lights a fire in the grove.

10

Safety Smar

Don't go in the bath without Mom and Dad.
It could be too hot, and that might hurt bad!

One day Brecker Bunny forgot his listening ears.
That happens when your age is just three years.

Safety Smart

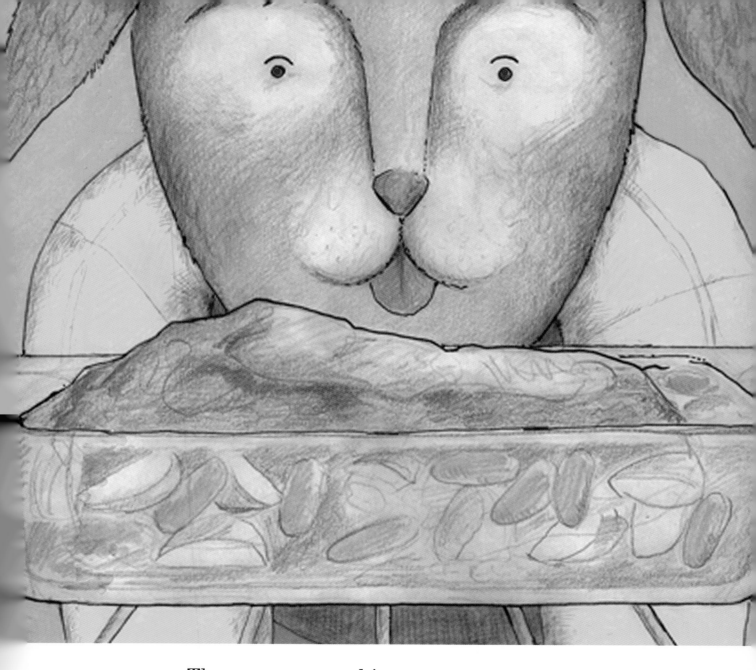

The oven was cooking a yummy roast.

"MMMM," Brecker thought. "I like roast the most."

13

So he opened the door to the oven alone.
He touched the pan. He started to groan.

Safety Smar

Never had his paws been so very sore.
He started to cry and sat on the floor.

Daddy came running to see what was wrong.
Mommy held Brecker and sang his favorite song.

Safety Smar

But nothing at home could make his burn better,
So an ambulance took him to the burn center.

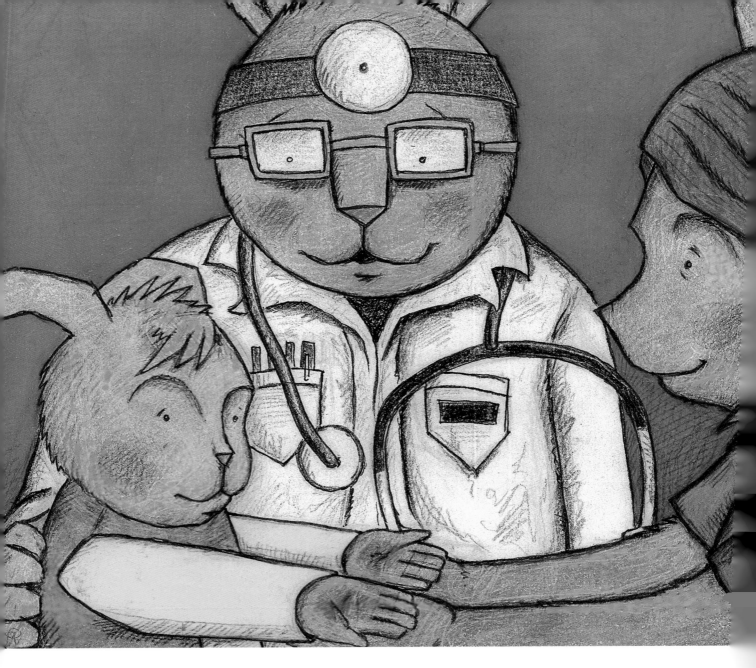

Here there were doctors and nurses who knew
How to make Brecker better, just what to do.

So they cleaned and wrapped his little paws
With lots of goop and bandages and gauze.

19

They took his temperature to see if he was sick,
And gave him medicine to make him better, "Ick."

Safety Smar

But he listened carefully to each doctor and nurse
Because he knew that they would stop his hurts.

21

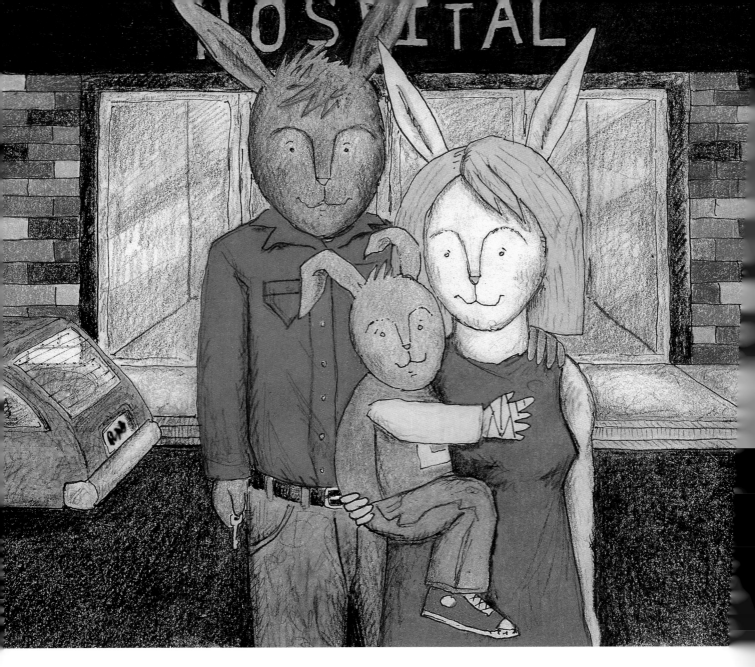

Mommy and Daddy stayed right by his side.
When it was time to leave they smiled really wide.

At home he will have to wear special clothes
To help his paws heal, as the new skin grows.

He'll have to do his exercises each and every day.
The doctor said that would make his paws okay.

Going home Brecker was glad for the help that he had.
He promised to listen because burns could hurt bad.

He still likes to jump and play and hop.
He still likes to twist and turn and bop.

He still has adventures up in his tree,
With Little Brother yelling, "Wait for me."

But there are some things that are just not fun.
Some adventures should be left undone.

When things are very hot you should stay away,
Or your paws and whiskers may not be okay.

Safety Smart!®

Be careful of boiling water on the stove,
Or when Farmer lights a fire in the grove.

30

Safety Smar

Don't go in the bath without Mom and Dad.
It could be too hot, and that might hurt bad!

Brecker learned his lesson and now tells others.
He even watches out for Little Brother.

Safety Smar

BRECKER BUNNY'S *Safety Smart!* TIPS

Instructions for Parents and Teachers:

Here are simple safety tips you can reinforce to help make your children Safety Smart! Champions. For more detailed tips, activities and discussion questions go to: **www.inspiredbyfamily.com.**

Page 4:
A tidy room is a safe room.

Page 6:
Never climb up what you can't climb down.

Page 7:
It is never too early to start talking to your child about safety.

Page 8:
Create a 3-foot 'safety zone' for children and pets around all camp fires, fireplaces and stoves.

BRECKER BUNNY'S *Safety Smart!* TIPS

Page 9:
Make sure pot and pan handles are always turned in to avoid accidental spills.

Page 10:
Use a candy or meat thermometer to test bath water. Bath water temperature should be between 90° - 100°F. (At 125°F, a standard setting, a child's skin can burn within 2 minutes. At 135°F a child's skin can burn in ten seconds and at 140°F, three seconds.)

Page 11:
Keep cooking area clean and clear of anything that can burn, such as, paper towels, potholders, curtains or food packaging.

Page 12:
Kids should never be left alone in a kitchen. One second can change your child's life forever.

Page 13:
Never wear long sleeves or loose clothing near a stove or oven. Brecker Bunny's sleeve could easily catch on fire! In case of an accident like this, take a moment to explain "Stop, Drop and Roll!"

BRECKER BUNNY'S *Safety Smart!* TIPS

Page 14:
Immediately put a burn, such as Brecker Bunny's, under cold water to stop any further damage to the skin. Then seek medical attention immediately.

Page 15:
*Protect your home by installing inter-connected smoke alarms and a home fire sprinkler system. For more information see **www.wafs.org** and **www.ul.com**.*

Page 19:
The ONLY safe medicine bottle is one that is out of a child's reach.

Page 28:
Notice the 3-foot perimeter of rocks set up around the camp fire.

Page 29:
Notice farmer has a water tanker at the ready, in case a fire would get out of hand.

BRECKER BUNNY'S *Safety Smart!* TIPS

Page 30:
Notice Brecker's mommy testing the water temperature with a meat thermometer.

Page 31:
Always keep a fully charged ABC fire extinguisher in the kitchen and garage. Use the PASS method: Pull (the pin); Aim (at the base of the fire); Squeeze (the trigger); and Sweep (the extinguisher from side to side). Ensure that everyone is being evacuated, that 911 has been called and that the environment is safe enough for an extinguisher attempt. If not...GET OUT!

Challenge kids to be like Brecker - be *Safety Smart!* champions - teaching their brothers and sisters, friends, and even their parents about fire safety.

SAFETY TIPS PROVIDED BY

Brecker Bunny's Family Calendar

Sunday	Monday	Tuesday	Wednesday	Thursday	Friday	Saturday
Remember to practice being *Safety Smart!*	1	2 **(October)** Prepare & practice home escape plan.	3	4 **(October)** Practice fire extinguisher PASS method (Pull Pin; Aim; Squeeze; Sweep) with all family members.	5	6 **(April & October)** Change Smoke & Carbon Monoxide Alarm batteries.
7 **(September)** Inspect furnace filter and schedule annual maintenance	8	9 Test Ground-Fault Circuit-Interrupters (GFCI's)	10	11 **(July)** Check water heater temperature setting, keep at 120° Fahrenheit	12	13 Make sure all extension cords are not pinched or overloaded. Throw away damaged or frayed cords.
14	15 Outfit unused wall outlets within children's reach with safety covers.	16	17 **(May)** Inspect air conditioning filter and schedule annual maintenance.	18	19 **(January)** Update emergency contact information.	20
21 **(January)** Update contents in First Aid Kit.	22	23 Test Smoke Alarms and Carbon Monoxide Alarms.	24	25 **(September)** Schedule home fire sprinkler inspection.	26	27 Inspect fire extinguisher as instructed on label.
28	29 Clean dryer exhaust duct.	30	31	**Incorporate these proactive fire prevention actions** into your daily routine & help keep your family fire-safe. On your family calendar copy the actions shown. Actions printed in black should be repeated every month. Actions printed in red should be performed once a year.		

For more information and updates please see **www.ul.com/consumers**, **www.ul.com/newsroom**, and **www.wafs.org**.

Brecker Bunny's Fire Safety Checklist

PREVENT - Many fires are caused by carelessness or by not noticing a seemingly minor, but potentially dangerous, situation. These fires easily can be prevented with education, common sense and planning. **That's where you come in!**

DO A SAFETY CHECK - Your mission is to go on a fire safety check around your home, looking for fire risk situations. Once you complete your checklist, find any "no" boxes that you checked. These risks need to be fixed immediately. **It's good to have you on the case!**

Look for these danger signs as you examine the rooms in your home:

 ALL ROOMS

ELECTRICAL CORDS & WIRES
Examine the cords on your electrical appliances like the television set, lamps, computer equipment, microwave oven and other appliances.

YES	NO	
☐	☐	Are all wires and cords in good repair?
☐	☐	Are wires and cords kept out from beneath furniture or carpets?
☐	☐	Are you sure there are no wires attached to walls

YES	NO	
		with staples or tacks that can damage the insulation?
☐	☐	Are outlets and extension cords carrying the proper electrical load as indicated on their rating labels? Be sure that you do not have more than one item plugged in to each individual outlet in your home - all it takes is one spark from an overloaded outlet to start a fire.

APPLIANCES

YES	NO	
☐	☐	Are electrical appliances like televisions, stereos and computer equipment well ventilated to avoid overheating?

HEATING DEVICES

YES	NO	
☐	☐	Are space heaters or other heating devices UL listed and always kept at least 3 feet away from anything?
☐	☐	Are heating devices placed on a flat, level floor to avoid tipping over?
☐	☐	Do you turn off portable heaters in bedrooms before going to sleep?
☐	☐	Is the furnace kept in good repair with filters replaced regularly?
☐	☐	Are heating vents kept clear, especially of flammable items like paper, boxes or clothing?

KITCHEN

STOVE

YES	NO	
☐	☐	When you cook, do you stay in the kitchen?
☐	☐	Is your stove clear of flammable items? Make sure there are no curtains, hanging cords, papers, trash or other flammables near the stove. Keep hot pads, papers and flammable items off the range.
☐	☐	Is the stove cleaned regularly to remove flammable grease buildup?
☐	☐	Is there a fire extinguisher within easy reach of the stove?
☐	☐	Are you careful not to wear loosefitting clothes that may catch fire by coming in contact with a burner?
☐	☐	Are all burners turned off when not in use?

APPLIANCES

YES	NO	
☐	☐	Are kitchen appliances unplugged when not in use?

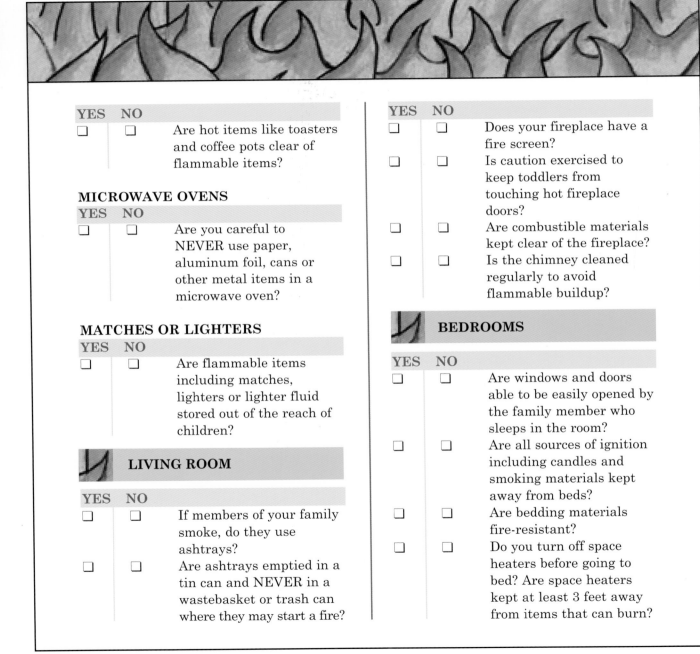

YES	NO	
☐	☐	Are hot items like toasters and coffee pots clear of flammable items?

MICROWAVE OVENS

YES	NO	
☐	☐	Are you careful to NEVER use paper, aluminum foil, cans or other metal items in a microwave oven?

MATCHES OR LIGHTERS

YES	NO	
☐	☐	Are flammable items including matches, lighters or lighter fluid stored out of the reach of children?

LIVING ROOM

YES	NO	
☐	☐	If members of your family smoke, do they use ashtrays?
☐	☐	Are ashtrays emptied in a tin can and NEVER in a wastebasket or trash can where they may start a fire?

YES	NO	
☐	☐	Does your fireplace have a fire screen?
☐	☐	Is caution exercised to keep toddlers from touching hot fireplace doors?
☐	☐	Are combustible materials kept clear of the fireplace?
☐	☐	Is the chimney cleaned regularly to avoid flammable buildup?

BEDROOMS

YES	NO	
☐	☐	Are windows and doors able to be easily opened by the family member who sleeps in the room?
☐	☐	Are all sources of ignition including candles and smoking materials kept away from beds?
☐	☐	Are bedding materials fire-resistant?
☐	☐	Do you turn off space heaters before going to bed? Are space heaters kept at least 3 feet away from items that can burn?